THE FIRST BOOK OF BARITONE/BASS SOLOS

PART III

compiled by Joan Frey Boytim

G. SCHIRMER, Inc.

DISTRIBUTED BY

HAL•LEONARD® CORPORATION

7777 W. BLUEMOUND RD. P.O. BOX 13819 MILWAUKEE, WI 53213

PREFACE

The First Book of Solos series has been compiled to meet requests of voice teachers who have expressed a need for more beginning vocal literature similar to the "Part I" and "Part II" books. This repertoire speaks to students who may have successfully sung songs from the *Easy Songs for Beginning Singers* series. Those students who have used *The First Book of Solos – Part I and Part II*, may still find that this level of song material is appropriate before venturing into the volumes of *The Second Book of Solos*. This new "Part III" may also suffice as a beginning book for certain students, or serve as a companion to "Part I" and "Part II." Since the level is the same for *The First Book of Solos – Part I, Part II and Part III*, a student can begin in any of the books.

The first two volumes were released in 1991 and 1993. Since then, some excellent songs have passed into the "Public Domain" category. It is significant that songs such as "The Green Cathedral," "Waters Ripple and Flow," "A Brown Bird Singing," "When I Think Upon the Maidens," "The Ships of Arcady," "May-Day Carol," and "The Time for Making Songs Has Come" have become available for young singers.

The anthologies in "Part III" contain 34 to 36 songs appropriate to specific voice types, and in suitable keys. The basic format provides songs of many styles from the baroque era into the 20th century. In addition to many familiar standard art songs, there are a number of unfamiliar gems, such as "The Bubble Song," the trilogy "At the Zoo," "Bluebird," "The Little Old Lady in Lavender Silk," "Maidens Are Like the Wind," "Sing a Song of Sixpence," and "When Big Profundo Sang Low C." In keeping with the original format, there are many American and British songs, as well as a good sampling of Italian, German and French art songs (with singable translations). Some favorites include "Invictus," "Come Back to Sorrento," "Vilia," and "I Walked Today Where Jesus Walked." As in the other books of the series, a few sacred solos are included. Many songs in "Part III" were previously obtainable in only sheet form or have been long out of print. In order to include songs represented by the 1916 to 1922 year span, several of the accompaniments and songs may prove to be a bit more of a challenge than in "Part I" and "Part II."

The First Book of Solos – Part III concludes this series of five books for each voice type, with no song duplication (*The First Book of Solos – Part I, Part II, Part III, The Second Book of Solos – Part I, Part II*). The number of songs in the twenty volumes totals 668. The average number of songs presented for each voice numbers approximately 167. This presents a wide smorgasbord of vocal literature for studio and performance use for student singers at most any age.

G. Schirmer is to be commended for allowing this series of vocal solos to grow substantially. Wherever I meet teachers who have used these many books, they express profound thanks for them, and acknowledge that their availability makes repertoire demands so much easier to manage. May you and your students enjoy the new choices made available in this anthology.

Joan Frey Boytim
June, 2005

CONTENTS

THE BEGGAR'S SONG

Richard Leveridge
(1670-1758)

Gaily

How — jol - ly are we beg - gars Who — nev - er toil for treas - ure; We — know no care but how — to share Each

BERGÈRE LÉGÈRE
(Capricious shepherd-maid)

English version by Sigmund Spaeth

Harmonized by
Jean-Baptiste Weckerlin
(1821-1910)

Un poco allegretto

Ber - gè - re Lé - gè - re, Je
Ca - pri - cious, De - li - cious, A -

crains tes ap - pas; ___ Ton â - me S'en - flam - me, Mais
dored shep - herd - maid, ___ You're charm - ing, Yet harm - ing My

tu n'ai - mes pas. ___ Ta mi - ne Mu - ti - ne
heart, I'm a - fraid. ___ In your face re - bel - ling,

to Mrs. G. Holmes Thomas

BLUE ARE HER EYES

Mary MacMillan

Wintter Watts
(1884-1962)

CAPTAIN MAC

P.J. O'Reilly

Wilfrid Sanderson
(1878-1935)

Oh, well set up and hand-some as a sail-or-man could be, Was
Cap-tain John Mac-pher-son of the schoon-er Ben Ma-chree!_ A

shy and mod-est bach - e - lor of just two score and ten— The

i - dol of the la - dies and the en - vy of the men!......

Oh,

East and West, North and South, 'Fris - co to Pe - rim,

Did-n't mat-ter where he went, the gals were af-ter him! They

chased him— pur-sued him— they would not let him be, Till

senza rall.

Cap-tain John Mac-pher-son cursed the day he went to sea!

silent.

He

senza rall.

Cap-tain John Mac-pher-son cursed the day he went to sea!

ff

Slower.
mp

At last he grew so

legato il basso.

cresc.

wea-ry that he said un-to the mate "Un-less this a-dor-

f strepitoso. ———

(indignantly.)

-a-tion stops, I'll go clean off my pate; Why can't the gals leave

f accel ———

me a-lone?" said the mate "I'll save you, sir!......... You take a wife, that's

my ad-vice, and leave the gals....... to her!".........

Oh, East and West, North and South,

'Fris-co to Pe-rim, Did-n't mat-ter where he went, the

COME, O COME, MY LIFE'S DELIGHT

Thomas Campion

Horatio Parker
(1863-1919)

The _ more en - joyed, the more di - vine, O come, _____ and take from

me The pain of be - ing de - prived of thee!

Thou all sweet-ness dost en - close, _____

THE COMPLACENT LOVER

Charles Selby

Horatio Parker
(1863-1919)

Cheerfully and rather fast

Phil-lis is my on-ly joy, Faith-less as the winds or seas,

Some-times cun-ning, some-times coy, Yet she nev-er fails _____ to

please; If with a frown,

CONSECRATION

Robert Franz
(1815-1892)

English version by Gertrude Tingley

EVENING

Thomas Merton*

John Jacob Niles
(1892-1980)

words____ that flow-er On____ lit - tle voi - ces, light as stems of lil - lies, stems of lil - lies. And

where blue heav -en's fad -ing fire last shines,_____ Re - flect-ed in the pop - lar's____

rip - ple, One lit - tle wake-ful bird, Sings like a show -er,

lit - tle wake-ful bird, Sings like a show -er,_____ like a show-er.

to John Coates

FIVE EYES

Walter de la Mare*

C. Armstrong Gibbs
(1889-1960)

*This poem used by kind permission of the Author

five eyes smould-'ring green _ and bright:

Squeaks from the flour-sack, squeaks from where The cold wind stirs on the

em-pty stair, Squeak-ing and scamp-'ring, ev - 'ry-where. Then

down they pounce, now _ in, now out, At whisk-ing tail, and _ snuff-ing snout; While

GEHEIMES
(The Secret)

Johann Wolfgang von Goethe

Franz Schubert
(1797-1828)

in die Run - de; doch___ sie sucht nur zu ver-
joy - ous greet - ing, *To___ him on - ly she dis-*

kün - - den ihm die nächs - te sü - ße
cours - es *Of their next de - light - ful*

Stun - de, ihm die nächs - te sü - ße___ Stun -
meet - ing, *Of their next___ de - light - ful meet -*

- de.
- ing.

GOD SO LOVED THE WORLD

from *The Crucifixion*

John 3:16, 17

John Stainer (1840-1901)
Arranged by William Stickles

to the Rev. Dr. Washington Gladden

HOW LONG WILT THOU FORGET ME

Psalm 13

Oley Speaks
(1874-1948)

lest   I   sleep____   the   sleep____ of the dead,

rall. -

lest____   I   sleep____   the   sleep of the dead.   Con -

- e - dim. - - to end

sid - er   and hear me,   oh Lord____ my God;   con -

sid - er   and hear   me,   oh Lord   my   God.

IN THE LUXEMBOURG GARDENS

Rêverie

Kathleen Lockhart Manning
(1890-1951)

The au-tumn leaves are fall-ing thro' the gar - - dens,

But in their heart is spring! I hear him mur - mur:

"Ah! je t'ai - - me!" As she an-swers low:

to Francis Rogers

INVICTUS

William Ernest Henley

Bruno Huhn
(1871-1950)

Out of the night that cov-ers me, Black as the pit from pole to pole, I thank what-ev-er gods may be For my ___ un-con-quer-a-ble soul. In the fell clutch of

straight the gate, How charged with pun - ish - ments the

scroll, I am the mas - ter

of my fate I am the

cap - tain _____ of my soul. _____

to Walter Creighton

IT WAS A LOVER AND HIS LASS

William Shakespeare

Roger Quilter
(1877-1953)

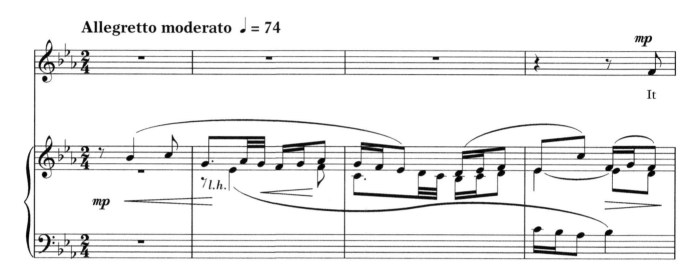

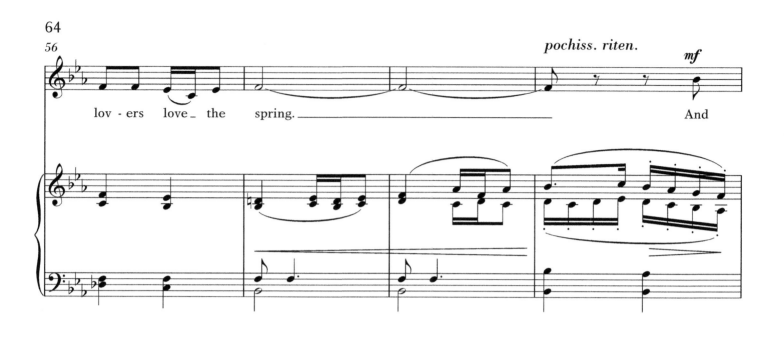

lov - ers love — the spring. _____ And

there - fore take the pre - sent time, With a hey, and a ho, and a

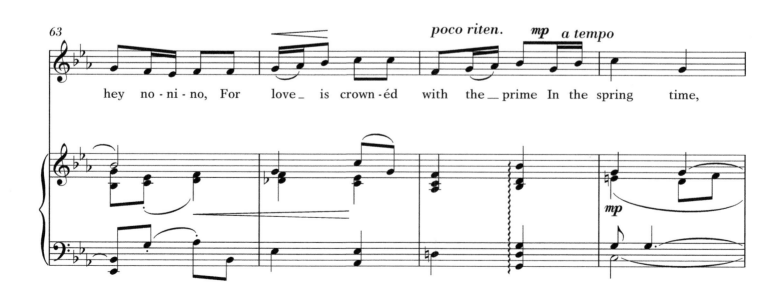

hey no - ni - no, For love — is crown - éd with the — prime In the spring time,

the on - ly pret - ty ring time, When

birds do sing, hey ding a ding, ding, ding a ding, ding,

ding a ding, ding; Sweet lov - ers love ___ the spring.

LET NOT YOUR HEART BE TROUBLED

John 14:1, 27

Oley Speaks
(1874-1948)

IO SO CHE PRIA MI MORO
(I vow my heart so troubled)

English version by Nathan Haskell Dole

Pancrazio Aniello

Largo assai

poco rit.

a tempo

Io
I

poco rall.

so che pria mi mo - ro che a - ver pa - ce e ri - sto - ro al
vow my heart so trou - bled Would glow with peace re - dou - bled, To

a tempo

cor — che lan - gue,
know — for cer - tain:

D.S. al Fine

LA MAISON GRISE
(The Grey House)

Arman de Caillavet and Robert de Flers
English version by Adrian Ross

André Messager
(1797-1856)

Andante

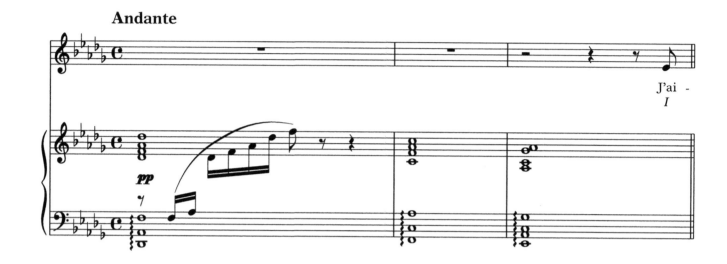

J'ai -
I

Andante tranquille

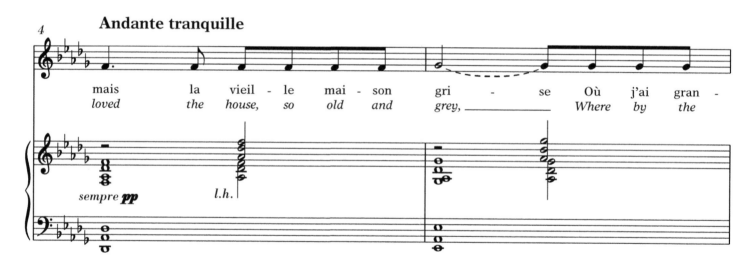

mais la vieil - le mai - son gri - se Où j'ai gran -
loved the house, so old and grey,_____ Where by the

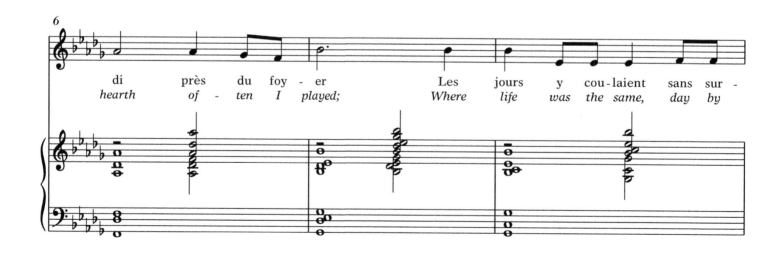

di près du foy - er Les jours y cou - laient sans sur -
hearth of - ten I played; Where life was the same, day by

MORIR VOGLIO
(That I might die)

Emanuele D'Astorga
(1681-1736)

D.S. al Fine

DER MUSIKANT
(The Musician)

Joseph von Eichendorff

Hugo Wolf
(1860-1903)

Wan-dern lieb ich für mein Le - ben, le-be e - ben, wie ich kann,
Oh what joy through life to wan - der; though I've nei - ther home nor wealth,

wollt ich mir auch Mü-he ge - ben, paßt es mir doch gar nicht an.
yet I know, though oft I pon - der: there's no wealth like sov - 'reign health.

29

Man - che Schö - ne macht wohl Au - gen, mei - net, ich ge -
Man - y a maid, if I would let her, glad - ly she would

32

fiel ihr sehr, wenn ich nur was woll - te tau - gen,
an - swer: Yea! if you'd learn a trade that's bet - ter

35

so ein ar - mer Lump nicht wär.
than to sing and play all day!

38

ONCE I LOVED A MAIDEN FAIR

Horatio Parker
(1863-1919)

QUE L'HEURE EST DONC BRÈVE
(How Brief Is the Hour)

Armand Silvestre
English version by Isabella G. Parker

Jules Massenet
(1842-1912)

RIVER-BOATS

Kathleen Lockhart Manning
(1890-1951)

Moderato ♩ = 104

A - long the quays the riv-er-boats are glid - ing, On the tide their dark shapes soft - ly rid - ing; They come and go so si - lent - ly and

slow,

The hearts that beat, the lives that ebb and flow,

cresc.

cresc.

meno mosso

a tempo

Where have they been, those boats? Where will they go?

A - long the quays the riv - er - boats are glid -

rall.

a tempo

ing.

DIE ROSE, DIE LILIE
(The rose and the lily)

Heinrich Heine
English version by Henry G. Chapman

Robert Franz
(1815-1892)

Allegretto con grazia

Die Ro - se, die Li - lie, die Tau - be, die Son - ne, die
The rose and the lil - y, the dove and the sun - light, I

liebt' ich einst al - le in Lie - bes - won -
loved them all once with a deep de - vo -

ne. Ich lieb' sie nicht mehr, ich
tion. I love them no more! I

to Madame Povla Frijsh

THE PASTURE

Robert Frost*

Charles Naginski
(1909-1940)

*From "Collected Poems" by Robert Frost. By permission of Henry Holt and Company, Publishers.

wait   to watch the   wa - ter   clear,_____   I   may):

I   sha'n't be gone   long.—   You   come too.

I'm go-ing out to   fetch   the lit - tle   calf   That's stand-ing   by   the

moth - er. It's so young, It totters when she

licks it with her tongue.

poco rall.

I sha'n't be gone long.— You come too.

p

poco rall.

DER SCHNEE IST ZERGANGEN
(The snow is all melted)

Wilhelm Osterwald

Robert Franz
(1815-1892)

to my mother
THE SEA-BIRD

Roger Quilter
(1877-1953)

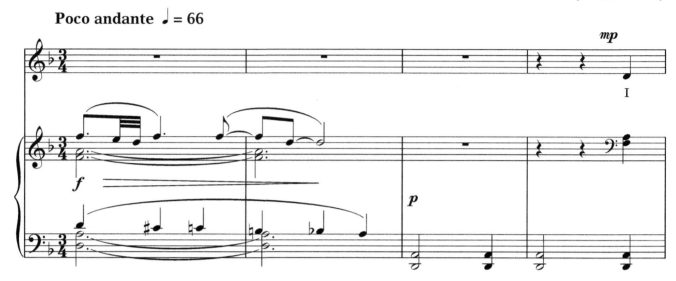

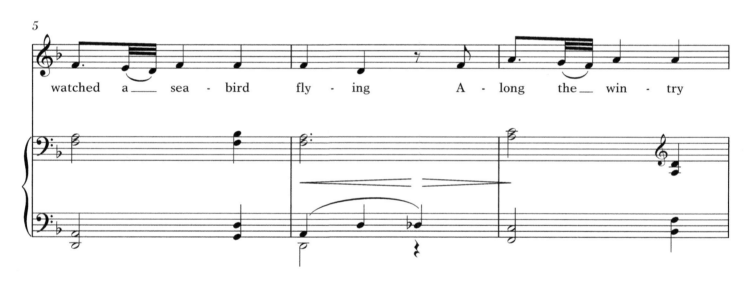

THE SHIPS OF ARCADY

Francis Ledwidge

Michael Head
(1900-1976)

I can hear the sail-ors' song From the blue edge _ of the sea,

Pass-ing like the lights a-long _ Through _ the dusk-y fil-i-gree. _

Then where moon and wa - ters meet

Sail _____ by sail they pass a-way, With

lit - tle friend - ly winds re-plete

Blow - ing from the break - ing day. _____

And when the lit - tle ships have flown, Dream - ing still of

38

Ar - ca - dy I look a - cross the waves, a - lone

colla voce

41 *rit.*

In the mist - y fil - i - gree.

poco rubato

44 *rit.*

p l.h.

r.h.

47 *pp a tempo*

Through the faint - est fil - i - gree

ppp

O - ver the dim _____ wa - ters go

Lit - tle ships of Ar - ca - dy

When the morn - ing moon is low.

THE SKIPPER

F.J. Dennet

W.H. Jude
(1851-1922)

1. A skip - per am I, no dan - ger can _____ My
2. But tho' _____ I love to brave the storm, _____ My

ar - dent, my ar - dent spir - it daunt, _____ As I guide my craft _____ o'er the
heart, _____ my heart with joy will beat _____ When from the deck _____ I _____

life___ is as free as the wind that blows,_____ For my home___ is
come___ what may, she'll ne'er be - tray,_____ Her___ skip - per up

rit. ad lib.   *a tempo*

on ___ the sea. Yo ho! yo ho!___ Then give___ me a right good craft and
on ___ the sea. Yo ho! yo ho!___

colla voce   *a tempo*

crew,_____ And I'll___ con - tent - ed be; For

SONG OF THE ARMOURER

Frances V. Hubbard

George B. Nevin
(1892-1943)

swings, And a heart_y song, both loud, gay and strong, To the tune thus the work_man sings.

Con animato

Oh, ring, ring mer_ri_ly steel on steel, The forge is glit_ter_ing bright, ___ As, with clang and with cling, thus I gai_ly sing, While the weap_ons I forge for fight. ___

kling, kling, kling and a klang, klang, klang, Keeping time with the tune I sing, Oh,

Con spirito

ring, ring mer _ ri _ ly, steel on steel, The forge is glit _ ter _ ing

bright,_____ As with clang and with cling thus I gai _ ly sing, While the

Grandioso

weap_ons I forge for fight._____

SPIRIT OF GOD

George Croly

William Harold Neidlinger
(1863-1924)

soul a - way.

Teach me to feel that Thou art al - ways nigh;

Teach me the strug-gles of the day to bear, To check the ris - ing

doubt, the reb - el sigh; Teach me the pa-tience of un - ceas - ing pray'r.

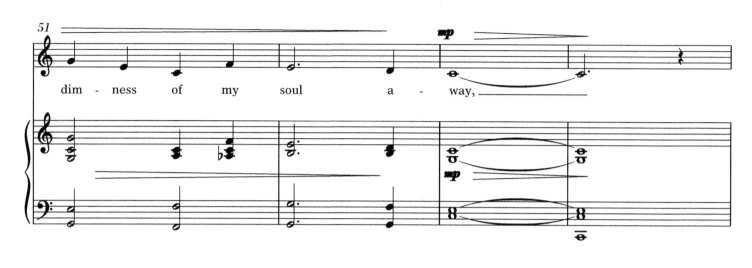

dim - ness of my soul a - way, _____

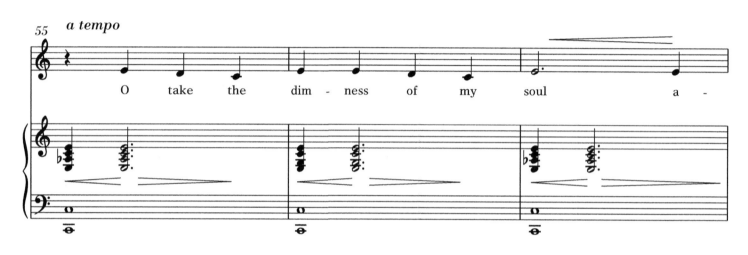

O take the dim - ness of my soul a -

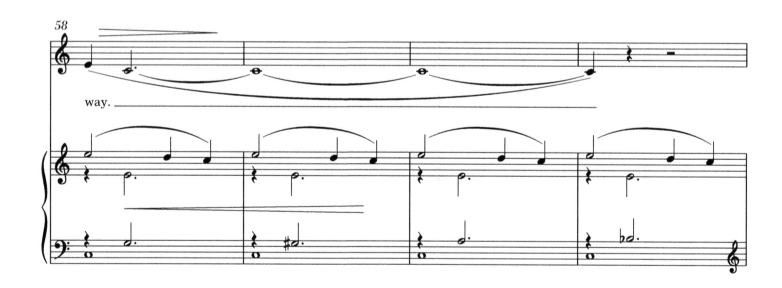

way. _____

THE TINKER'S SONG

Charles Dibdin
(1745-1814)

Pomposo

1. A Tink - er I am, my __ name's Nat-ty Dan, From morn till night I
   man of war, the __ man at the bar, Phy - si - cians, priests and

trudge it; So low is my fate, My __ pers-'nal es - tate Lies
think - ers, That rove up and down Great __ Lon - don town, __

to Gladys Harris

TRUSTING IN THEE

Claude L. Fichthorn

Con moto

Oft have I wan - dered, strayed far from Thee;

Yet hast Thou ev - er watched o - ver me. In night's en - cir - cling gloom,

in bright-est days, Thy love shall fol - low me, in all my

ways.

WHEN ALL NIGHT LONG A CHAP REMAINS

from *Iolanthe*

W.S. Gilbert

Arthur Sullivan
(1842-1900)

PVT. WILLIS:

1. When

all night long   a chap   re-mains,   On sen - try-go, to chase mo -
in that House   M. P.'s   di - vide,   If they've   a brain and cer - e -

not - o - ny   He ex - er - cis - es   of his brains,   That
bel - lum, too,   They've got   to leave   that brain   out - side,   And

WHEN BIG PROFUNDO SANG LOW "C"

Marion T. Bohannon

George Botsford
(1874-1949)

fun - do When he sang a song Though his voice was big and strong It was

full of sym - pa - thy And of him 'tis said That he

woke up all the dead When he sang down to low "C"_____ When Big Pro -

fun - do sang low "C" All the la - dies they would

quiv - er For the great big note that came from his throat seemed to

make the tim - bers shiv - er He could make you cry He could

make you sigh With _ sim - ple mel - o - dy   For he

sang with a will And your heart stood still When Big Pro - fun - do sang low

opt. "C"   Way   down   down   to   low __ "C."

WHEN I WAS ONE-AND-TWENTY

Alfred Edward Housman

Arthur Somervell
(1863-1937)